Living Well: Caring Enough To Do What's Right

ISBN: 1-4392-4146-5
ISBN-13: 9781439241462

To order additional copies, please contact us.
BookSurge
www.booksurge.com
1-866-308-6235
orders@booksurge.com

Living Well: Caring Enough To Do What's Right

A Guide to a Great Life and World

Joseph M. Furner

Publisher

2009

Dedication/In Memory/Thanks

This book is dedicated to my mother, Catherine Mae Duquette Furner, who I love so much. She has been my role model and the peacemaker in our family. She has always cared enough to do what is right by all her children, always teaching us to be good people. May God bless her always. Thanks Mom for all your love and support. I would also like to recognize the memory of Mestiza Furner; she loved to play, eat, sleep, and be by my side as I worked on the computer at all times. She brought many years of love and happiness into my life and the life of Esperanza; may she rest in peace and may we meet again in our eternal resting places. A special thanks to many wonderful people and my family members, people like Carlos, Barbara, Robin, Juan, Deb, Sue, and Scott to name a few, that have crossed my path in life and have influenced me in positive ways to grow and be a better person, helping me to care enough to do what is right.

Chapters

1. Introduction   1

2. Attitude is Everything   5

3. Peace: Interior and in the World   9

4. Service to All your Fellow Men—We Need to Love Each Other   17

5. Take Ego Out of Your Life   23

6. Pray, Whether it is Using the Torah, Koran, Bible, Rosary, Prayer Beads, or Yoga, etc.   31

7. Have High Standards, Strive for the Best, Don't Settle for Mediocrity   39

8. Live Life, Read Books, Watch Movies and TV, Some of the Best Movies, Books and TV to Lift your Spirit   51

9. The 10 Commandments-Keep Focused on God and Heaven—Don't Get Consumed by this Earth, your Ego, Materialism, and Competition, etc.   61

10. The Living Well Prayer   69

"I pray that I may care enough, to love enough,
to share enough, to let others become what they can be."
-John O'Brien

Chapter 1
Introduction

Conduct yourselves with reverence during the time of your sojourning.
-1 Peter 1:17

This booklet/libretto has been a work in progress as I journeyed through my life. So many lessons are being learned on a daily basis, and Earth is our school. A lot of personal learning occurs to all of us in this world daily as we go about living each day. We learn each day about life by the people with whom we interact with and through the consequences of our own irresponsible behavior often times. It is important for all of us to live in Spirit with our higher power and know we are put here on Earth for a mission and a purpose; we are here to serve each other and fulfill the mission of our God and Source. In a time now in the 21st century, we are starting to feel a great deal of chaos, lawlessness, wars, fighting over religious differences, and strife in the world. So many even live without any regard for our laws or could care less about whether they toss litter on the ground, run a stop sign, act aggressively toward someone in public like at the supermarket, or show no respect for themselves while sporting public intoxication or risking the life of another driver by driving drunk. *Living Well: Caring Enough to do What's Right* is a book of reflection for all of humanity on rethinking how we live our lives; how we respect others and ourselves; how we react and interact with our fellow human beings; and how we respect and take care of our mother Earth. In an age of greed and corruption, there is not usually a day that goes by when we don't hear about some elected official or leader who is under scrutiny for fraud or taking a bribe. Many elected officials do things more discretely, voting a particular way on an issue to support big business or a developer over what their constituents want or support. They do this to guarantee themselves campaign funding and other perks. Employees hiring workers under the table or avoiding paying the correct taxes and insurance for their employees or people avoiding paying their fair share of taxes by working under the table.

One can go on and on with examples in our society today of people being dishonest or not abiding by our laws and codes, or not tithing or paying into the system so that our world will function with some law and order, often times forgetting why we even have such rules and laws. All of this dishonesty, greed, and corruption only lead to a chaotic, lawless, care-less civilization. We need to remember why we are all here; we are all God's children, and we must love and respect our fellow human beings, whether or not they are from the same race, religion, family, etc. We must all learn to cooperate, collaborate, and get along with each other in a civilized, loving way. This booklet is about all of that; it is about how we need to live our lives so we can all live here on Mother Earth together, where we all care enough to do what is right, which ultimately affects each of us individually, as well as our country, our race, our group, our environment, and our very existence on Gaia (Earth). As the famous American prophet Edgar Casey believed, we really must live in the present; we need to look at how we relate to others and our planet and take care of each other so as to ensure a sound future for us and future generations. I pray that this book will touch the lives of so many so that it will touch the lives of humanity in striving to make our world a better place for all of us, and creating a world of peace. May God bless you always. God has so many blessings he wants to give to each one of us; all we need to do is ask. I enjoyed the book by Bruce Wilkinson, *The Prayer of Jabez*; I love the message and prayer. I think we can say the prayer singularly, but I think personally we should consider saying it plurally as humans as follows:

And Jabez called on the God of Israel saying,
"Oh, that You would bless us indeed,
And enlarge our territories,
that Your hand would be with us all as your children,
and that You would keep us from evil,
that we may not cause pain to each other!"

-From 1 Chronicles 4:10

Please feel free to read that little book on Jabez; I thought the prayer was beautifully explained in the book. The first thing mentioned is "you would bless me indeed." As explained in the book, God wants to give us all many blessings; all we need to do is ask him for them. When Jabez says "enlarge my territory," he means enlarge my territory to do thy work of the Lord; I think this is beautiful. The rest is more self-explanatory; that the Lord's hand be with you always and keep one from evil and that you may not cause pain to other people. Jabez was very humble in his prayer, as explained in the book. I think you would really like the book; I hope you like the Prayer of Jabez and consider saying the plural version for ALL of US. By the way, Jabez was

3

the name of my father's grandfather, my great grandfather; he came from East Sussex, England. There is a town there named Furner's Green. My friend, Robin, took me there when I went to England a few years ago. Well, may God bless you always; feel free to read on......There is a song I have heard before; some of the lyrics are: "This is your life, are you who you want to be?" We must all answer this question and consider the following: are we living are lives with rectitude? Are we happy with who we are? Do we care enough about our fellow human beings and world to do what is right? Are you who you want to be? Then as I said, read on.....and hopefully you will become a better you.

Key Idea from this Chapter:

Do as the quote says; conduct yourself with reverence during your life's journey here on this planet. Remember reverence and integrity. Treat others as you would want to be treated. Care enough to do what is right, as it may be what is right for all our fellow human beings.

Chapter 2
Attitude is Everything

*"I thank God for my handicaps, for, through
them, I have found myself, my work, and my God."*
-Helen Keller

We have all heard the phrase, "Attitude is Everything."
Well, I think this is true; it is all about attitude and how we
react to things in life. Humans certainly are not perfect; we react in a negative, greedy, hateful, vengeful, or maybe mean way
sometimes. We often are all so busy working to get more in life,
to compete with our classmates for the highest test score, or to
drive a prestigious car, or wear the best or most famous designer
clothes or to have a nose job that looks like a famous actor, we all
want to move up the ladder of success, sometimes not thinking
about our attitudes and how it may rub off on others. One of my
all time famous quotes about attitude is from Charles Swindall
as follows:

> "The longer I live, the more I realize the impact of at-
> titude on life. Attitude, to me, is more important than
> facts. It is more important than the past, than education,
> than money, than circumstances, than failures, than suc-
> cesses, than what other people think or say or do. It is
> more than appearance, giftedness, or skill. It will make
> or break a company...a church...a home. The remark-

> able thing is we have a choice everyday regarding the
> attitude we will embrace for that day. We cannot change
> the past...we cannot change the fact that people will act
> in a certain way. We cannot change the inevitable. The
> only thing we can do is play on the one string we have,
> and that is our attitude...I am convinced that life is 10%
> what happens to me and 90% how I react to it. And so it
> is with you...we are in charge of our Attitudes."

I really like this quote by Charles Swindall; it is a good thing to keep in mind that 90% of our Attitude is how we react to things. If we can just not allow ego to interfere; if we could hold back on the anger and ridicule, think about the possibilities. Always we must act with love and kindness; God knows we must act firmly sometimes with certain people or situations, but we can do it in a loving sort of way. War and hate are not the solutions; we must work toward peace in all cases, as there is no way to peace. Peace is the way. As we are talking about percentage, maybe some have heard about the 80:20 Principle, where some believe that 20 percent of the people on earth do 80 percent of all the work. If we could just get all people on board doing their fair share, maybe we might have less stress in this world for all of us. We must create a new vision, a new world, a world where all people care enough to do what is right. The whole earth is full of God's glory; we must celebrate this everyday. We must celebrate this by having the best attitude possible in our lives.

Our attitudes toward how we listen to God are important. I am reminded of Padre Pio of Pietrelcina of Italy and his thoughts on spiritual guidance and our attitudes. He says we can always distinguish what comes from the heart and is inspired by God, and what is inspired by the devil. He felt that the Spirit of

God is a Spirit of peace, and even in cases of grave sin, it makes us feel tranquil, sorrowful, humble, and confident. This is due precisely due to "His mercy." The spirit of the demon, on the other hand, excites, exasperates, and makes us in our sorrow feel something like anger against ourselves, whereas our first charity must be to ourselves, and so if certain thoughts bother you, this agitation never comes from God, who gives tranquility, being the Spirit of Peace. We need to keep this in mind as we go about our daily interactions and listen closely to God in us speaking with love, mercy, and tranquility as we are confronted with issues, feel God's peace as he directs you, and as he helps you to react and behave outward, to have an attitude based on peace.

As we all know, each person is dealt a deck in life, or makes their own bed and has to sleep in it, but really, attitude is everything; it is all about how we react to things. I applaud people born into this world with disabilities or who are born gay. Whether black, Muslim or Jew, or a woman raised in a strict Catholic family, we must all realize we each have been given a cross to bear so to speak and must journey through life the best we can, with the very best attitude, being kind to others, knowing God loves us, he cares, he forgives us for all our sins, and we are all part of a greater loving mission, a mission from God. If you have God in your life, everyday will be filled with hope. This is the attitude we all need to carry with us like Helen Keller did.

Key Idea from this Chapter:

Attitude is everything; be careful how you react to people and situations. Count to ten before reacting. There is always a kind way to deal with any situation; try to find it. Our very attitudes can bring about peace. Attitude is usually 90% of how we react to things.

Chapter 3
Peace: Interior and in the World

"Lord, make me an instrument of Your peace!"
-St. Francis of Assisi

We have all heard statements like, "Blessed are the peace-makers for they shall be called sons of God." If we all as humans here on earth work toward peace and are kind and loving to one another, we are doing Allah's work. "My peace I give unto you" from John 14:27 is a powerful message from which we all need to take heed. The peace of our Lord and acting on it can make our world the best it can be. Some contend that there is no way to peace, that peace must be the way. I like this argument; we all must be peacemakers here on this planet. It must start with each one of us individually. If we truly want interior peace and world peace, we must all live and react peacefully and lovingly toward our fellow human beings; we must work out our differences and negative feelings toward others or nations, but do it in the harmony of God in us. God is in all of us, and is called Emmanuel.

Unfortunately, greed, selfishness, and materialism get in the way of peace here on earth. If we could all only realize that, would we want to go down in history as a peacemaker or some-

Joseph M. Furner

one who insisted on wars and the murder of thousands or millions of people? Do we want to be known as people like Mother Theresa of Calcutta, who helped the poor in India, St. Theresa, who stood up for her convictions to turn around the Catholic Church and make us closer to our God, like Martin Luther King, who peacefully fought for equal rights for blacks and all individuals, or like Gandhi, who wanted peace and equality for all people in a non-violent way. Also known as "Ahimsa." We all need to use an Ahimsa approach to living, a peaceful approach to solving all our problems without fighting or using physical aggression. Throughout history, there have been many leaders of peace, people who everyday acted from within to create world peace and never strived for a medal of honor or reverence, while there have been as many who used their power, ego, and influence to harm and kill populations, not allowing for equality for all human individuals. People have used the bible, Torah, and Koran, and many of our sacred books and scriptures to twist the truth to manipulate why it was okay to hurt or stop some group of people, be it for their color, gender, sexuality, etc. to not allow them the same rights afforded to them as others may have. It is disturbing to many to this day to say things like the USA is such a great nation and/or democracy, yet the founders who came here worked to eliminate an already existing population of people, the American Indians, indigenous to those lands for many years, killing off and still discriminating against indigenous populations even today in the 21st century.

I had a chance to live in Mexico for four years. I also traveled throughout Guatemala. I was shocked to see the level of discrimination that still exists today, the name calling, the inability for them to move up to better jobs and a better way of life,

10

all due primarily due to the color of their skin. It is sad, but the truth sometimes is sad, and if we as humans that have the ability to do something about it can, we should; we should work toward peace this way. Can't we co-exist, as people of color, people of varying religions, and people of differing sexualities?

Interior peace begins with oneself; it begins with one knowing who he or she is and knowing his or her faith and his or her love for God or supreme source. We must find this first before we can work out and achieve world peace; it only takes a handful of people to achieve this. We all know what it is like when someone is kind to us, when another takes the time to talk, to answer a question, to guide us, to smile, to assist, to care; we know how we feel when we come across someone who was like this to us sometime in our lives. Has the world really gotten that busy, and that materialistic, that we have become so consumed by how we react to others in a hasty, unkind, and uncaring way? We must take each day that we are on this earth as a day that we are in school, to learn from others of what is right and what is wrong, how we felt and what emotions are expelled. Did you feel used by someone? Did you feel they really didn't care when they were checking you out at the cash register or in the bank? Did someone bump into you in their mad rush to get to the last seat on the bus without any regard to how the box they were carrying banged up and hurt your arm? Are we all really in that much of a hurry to get somewhere or get something that we do not need to be and act in a peaceful way? While it certainly may not be easy, it starts with each one of us; it starts with educating our selves and caring enough to do what is right. We must teach our young people to care and to be honest, ethical, caring individuals to take care of all of the people of mother earth. Teach people to

Joseph M. Furner

respect themselves enough not to fall into the traps of addictions of drugs, alcohol, sex, gambling, etc. which in turn hurt family members and loved ones. I have had the chance to live in Colombia for a few years and being that my spouse is Colombian, go there regularly.

I am sad to see the people in such a beautiful country living now the way they must with fear of the drug cartel and armies that have taken over, preventing growth and security where there is a lack of jobs and tourism due to safety issues, where there is a lack of hope, a country with beautiful people, scenery, fruits, music, and culture, a people with a 'heart" feeling oppressed due to the stigma of the drug situation. With such a demand for drugs in the USA, Europe, and other so called developed countries, this has brought a country that could have peace to a stand still for years, with insecurity and a lack of development due to the lack of control of the power of these armies and drug cartels. Who is to blame? Is it the greed of the people selling the drugs in Colombia, often times, people of big name, family, and stature hidden by layers of farms and names? Is it the blame of the people who find the need to consume such drugs in the USA and other developed countries? Do they realize that by consuming these drugs, they are hurting a country and are not allowing it to develop and reach its full potential, as well as not allowing it to have the peace it deserves? This may be so for other Asian countries in Afghanistan as well for the same need for opium and other drugs? Have some groups oppressed others intentionally so they can prosper and be the "Developed Countries," while others have to be called or remain as "the third world?"

Living Well: Caring Enough To Do What's Right

Many people are against guns, arms, and wars; many of these people feel that peace will never be gained if we as a world continue to use them against each other for personal, political, our state gains. It is ironic in a world where the supposed "civilized or developed" countries create the most advanced and destructive arms in the world, maiming innocent people using these so called anti-personal mines or bombs, how mean or cruel can such developed or civilized people or country be to innocent children of our most high God? In the Tao Te Ching, written more than 2500 years ago, I really admire the verses 30 and 31 that talk about living without force and weapons. The Tao contends that weapons often turn upon the wielder. The Tao also says all decent men detest weapons and violence, and that arms serve evil. I believe this to be true. Guns and wars only create more animosity and only later in life bring about more vengefulness. When force is used, it prompts resentment and revenge; these become the way to respond. Younger generations have ill feelings toward the takers of lives of parents and loved ones; it is all a vicious cycle that never brings a happy ending. We must work together; we must learn to cooperate, not compete. We are one world, and one people; we all need each other for us all to survive here on this Terra. It is saddening when the so called developed or civilized countries hold all the power, not allowing other countries to even use nuclear power, yet they are allowed to have sites that house nuclear arms and weapons of mass destruction themselves; they must have all the power as if they were the only good in this world. I think instead these so called developed and civilized countries should heed the advice from the Tao and be examples, doing away with even the most remote possibility of responding with such weapons of mass destruction.

Joseph M. Furner

Perhaps instead of seeing our countries as separate entities, we need to look at our world as one, break down all walls and borders, help each other, and work together for the betterment of all humankind, for people who all love and worship the very same God.

Peace is an extremely complicated concept. I have often been amazed that many of these so called "developed countries" can send rockets to outer space and the moon, can create vaccines and drugs to cure illnesses, can create the Internet, and all the advancing technologies we now have in this day and age, but no one can find a solution of world peace, a concept which almost seems like it should be easier to resolve than medical or technological advances. I have come to the conclusion that if any of us want peace on this earth, it must begin with ourselves first; we must remove our egos, our want for power, money, materialism, and fame and try to live first, always acting and reacting in a peaceful manner. God-centered living is what brings us peace. There may be a battle ground in our hearts for "more, more, more," more money, more power, more material things and more and important titles, but none of this, in the long term, will bring us peace. Often, positions of power bring compromising situations and greed and temptation, more work, and more frustration; we all need to repent and confess of our sins, change of our ways, and live in the ways of God which can lead us to a true peace of mind. Achieving peace in this world is a challenge; unfortunately, ego, poor communication, and lack of compromise tend to interfere with achieving peace. I will save the problems of poor communication and unwillingness to compromise for my next book as they are certainly big issues that interfere with all of us as humans getting along. We do need to learn how to better communicate with each other and to be able to compromise as well. We need to respect each other's differing view points and beliefs and be willing to give and take occasionally. If we see an inequality in the world, we need to work toward changing this, but peacefully; if it is in us to work toward this with such a great passion like Martin Luther King did and it brings us to our death, then we did not die in vain. Doing it peacefully is the way. Martin Luther King did not do what he did to gain personal fame; he did it for a group of people as he saw an injustice, an inequality, that needed to be addressed. Thankfully his work has paved the way to much, but still not enough, equality for a race of people worldwide. Peace can be brought about by how we manage it or decide to manage it, for that matter. That is, if we all are conscientious of it. If we really want world peace, "then let it begin with me;" this is the attitude we all must have, as cited by St. Francis of Assisi. Thomas Aquinas sums up the concept of peace best; he said, "True Peace consists in not separating ourselves from the will of God." Thomas Merton sums it up well with his quote, "We are not at peace with others because we are not at peace with ourselves, and we are not at peace with ourselves because we are not at peace with God." We are all searching for and deserving of great peace. I recall a preacher that once said, "Peace on the outside comes from knowing God from within." If we all want peace in our lives and in the world, we need to accept God and live in Spirit. Marianne Williamson says that, "Only by finding the love within us can we provide the love that will save the world. Let peace begin with each one of us everyday of our lives, let peace be our way of life.

Key Idea from this Chapter:

Start with finding your own form of interior peace, if it is through your faith, religion, prayers, counseling, or overcoming an addiction. Once you have inner peace, project this to others and the world around you in a way you know is right and ethical; others will learn from and react to your actions. Handle your problems and the injustice around you in a peaceful way, not with guns and wars, but rather with words and peace marches; try not to judge others, but show them why their actions may be hurtful to others. We all must work toward peace; we need to communicate better and be willing to compromise occasionally. We all must live by the philosophy, "let world peace begin with 'me.'"

Chapter 4

Service to All Your Fellow Men and Women—Love Each Other

"We must be the change we want to see in the world."
-Gandhi

"Here I am Lord, here I am, I come to do your will." We must remember this phrase from a song; we are all put on this Earth to do "God's will." We are not in as much control of our lives as we would like to believe. Turn your life over to God and do His will; go with His flow down the river of life. He will guide you and your life will be even better. Life is really about service to our fellow human beings and our world in which we live in. As Leo Tolstoy once said, "The vocation of every man and woman is to serve other people." I think this is a beautiful concept; it would be great if all humans adopted this philosophy for living. We live in one world; we must learn to take care of it and look out for each other. We really need to start showing more mercy for each other and our planet earth. I saw a picture

Joseph M. Furner

and video once of a homeless man along with a dog, cat, and a rat, all together getting along with each other and co-existing as they lay there together. Why is it that people alone seem to have such problems with getting along in this world and co-existing, always looking for a fight, or who is right, or which one has more of an ego? If we want to experience true happiness in life, we must serve others. Albert Schweitzer once said, "One thing I know: the only ones among you who will be really happy are those who will have sought and found how to serve."

Today we live in a world with a great deal of discrimination and hatred. There is jealousy, competition, and envy. Power struggles, corruption, and greed seem to rule the world. Whether countries or individuals, many people just want to keep gaining more for themselves without caring about on whom they step or of whom they take advantage in the process. People look down on others like the poor, the addicted, the uneducated, the illegal immigrants, and the disadvantaged like gays, disabled, and even still people with dark colored skin. People with HIV and AIDS are shamed in most parts of the world, yet, in Africa and many other parts of the world, there continues to be high rates of this disease and still little help for people who have this disparaging disease. None of this is right or fair. No person should be judged by his or her skin color, sexuality, gender, education, etc. As Martin Luther King said, "judge all, only be the content of their character."

It is sad that in this day and age, many of us would prefer to laugh at or judge others in their times of failure, whether it is our boss being fired for doing something unethical, a falling corrupt political leader, a child falling on his bike, a friend being caught

18

in a lie or scam, or a close friend or family member who cannot find a job. Instead of laughing at their shortcomings or failures, we should be praying for them and having feelings of renewed success for them, that they get that job, learn how to finally ride that bike, or repent from their sins and corrupt/unethical acts to then maybe rise up to be a better leader and person. Many times we as humans want to see others fail so that our insecurities don't look so bad in comparison. I think this is a flawed way of looking at others and the world. We should be praying for goodness; we should be helping people rise up to reach their full potential and to be the best they can be while on this planet, and not judging them or making them less superior to you and the norm. God is in all of us, even in the supposed most evil person born here on earth. The jails around the world are filled with people that need our prayers and support more than anywhere. What do we live for if not to make the world less difficult for each other? We need to know that God is in every person; some people unfortunately have allowed ego and this materialistic world in which we live to take a stronger hold on their lives, causing them to act out inappropriately, and to live without the Spirit of God within them. We must pray for all these people that Spirit takes a stronger hold in all of us, as we are all subject to temptation here on earth, and to error on the wrong side of the track. Our service to our fellow human beings is to pray for them, to love them, to respect them, and for all of us to be responsible for each other and our planet as one world.

I have always loved this quote by Gurdjieff: *"If you help others, you will be helped, perhaps tomorrow, perhaps in one hundred years, but you will be helped. Nature must pay off the debt...It is a mathematical law and all life is mathematics."* Since I was a math

19

teacher for many years and then a mathematics education professor at a big state university, I have always felt this to be true. One thing teachers have going for them is their service work to others. Every day, as educators, we get to help young people like math and know how to do it, be good people, and turn light bulbs on, so to speak. Teachers do a lot in this world to educate our youth, not just in the academic areas, but also to teach values and to be good people, and to make positive contributions to our world. Often nurses, doctors, lawyers, police, and others also have this same opportunity; they are employed in service related jobs with many benefits. It is not just the money. Many teachers or police officers may complain about the small wages they earn, but many say they would not trade their profession for anything in the world, as the rewards are so much more than any money can give you. When you help others, you are helping yourself feel good as well. In John Bunyan's book, *Pilgrim's Progress* he states, "You have not lived today until you have done something for someone who can never repay you." Perhaps as humans in our journey to heaven, maybe we need to always keep this in mind, we must serve others without wanting anything in return.

I do volunteer work at one of the senior centers near to where I live; I have done this for about twelve years now. Every Friday, I go and serve the people; I talk and listen to them, play bingo, clean, teach English, eat, and feel a part of their lives. Most of the people are low-income and Cubans. I enjoy going and speaking Spanish with them and helping them. Many are all alone in this world, with little or no family left to look after them, they have lost husbands or wives and in many cases, are sad and lonely. I love when I can go there each Friday to bring a little joy to their lives, to smile and listen, and to talk and serve them their meal. It is so rewarding. I think a movement of volunteerism is warranted around the world; when people volunteer and serve others, they feel better about who they are. When they give of themselves, when they put their needs aside to help their fellow human beings, it makes what God put us on this earth to do feel so right. God didn't put us here to accumulate wealth, degrees, or material goods. He wants us to serve our fellow humans to show love, compassion, and kindness every chance we get. What is better? When you die, for your tomb stone to read either: (1) made a million Euros, published 200 articles and books, and traveled the world, but always too busy to go to church or help others in need or (2) was kind to someone in need when they were dying? Winston Churchill once said, "We make a living by what we get, but we make a life by what we give." Recently, I saw a nice story about a lady from Santa Clara, Ecuador; her name was Sister Guillermina Gavilanes. She was serving her community every day, even at the age of 80 years old. She was a nurse and went around her village helping the sick and the poor, a real modern day saint, in my opinion. Sister Guillermina said she didn't want any statues or special recognitions, although all the village people said she does more for the community than even the mayor; she really cares and loves her fellow human beings. She said, " man should be of service to each other." She lives by this philosophy daily; she serves all with love. She deserves a salute here.

We need more people in this world like Sister Guillermina. Spenheim once said, "They are the true disciples of Christ, not who know most, but who love most." We must "carve our names on hearts, not on marble" as C.H. Spurgeon reminds us. We all need to pray and ask God to give and maintain in us "a heart of flesh to replace the heart of stone," as only such a heart can truly love.

We must stop letting consumerism and this material world run and ruin our lives. We need to stop getting involved in this rat race of driving faster, making more money, or getting to the top first. We are put on this earth to love each other, all people. To love our brothers and sisters, our mother-in-laws, the illegal immigrants, the poor, the disabled and even the gays is what we need to do. "To err is human, to forgive is divine" says Alexander Pope; I think that God wants us to judge less and love and forgive more. To be of service to our fellow earthlings should be our goal. A German Proverb says, "When one helps another, both are strong." Lastly, as Inez Francis contends, "It is better to light one candle than to curse the darkness, be the paschal candle for others, plant and cultivate hope."

Key Idea from this Chapter:

To put your ego aside and to serve your fellow man is what is important in life. Put materialism, the need for money and living in this rat race of our consumer/materialistic world aside and start seeing who really needs our help and what we can do for others. When we help others we are really helping ourselves feel better too. God created a world here of service to fellow humans. Service is our ultimate goal. We need to love and serve the world more and learn to forgive and judge less.

Chapter 5
Take Ego Out of Your Life

"Too much ego, too little humility."
-Rev. William N. Seifert, *Medjugorje Forum*

Too often, we allow our needs, our power, and our wants to be put in front of those of others or our planet. Many in this world have become consumed with materialism and having more and more stuff. We want tattoos and piercings; we want Mercedes Benz cars or fancy sports cars or yachts. We want name brand sneakers like Nike and other fancy name-brand clothes. Many young people in our world have Attention Deficit Disorder (ADD), while young kids might have this problem in school with sitting in school with their peers to learn and listen to the teacher. Many young adults have this same problem; they seek attention by blasting their loud music in the cars they drive, or by wearing outrageous clothing, piercings, pink hair, or doing whatever it takes to seek attention. They are deficit in attention and will strive to any length so that others will look at them or give them a second of their attention. Our egos seem to really need to be fed. We use whatever we can to seek attention to ourselves. Dr. Wayne Dyer talks about this in his book, *Inspirations*, how EGO means edging God out. I think this is true; we have

Joseph M. Furner

become too consumed by our own selves and what we want out
of life without considering the other several billion people on this
earth with us. We forget that there are huge amounts of poverty
and people dying all over the world due to starvation, AIDS,
and other maladies. It is sinful and heartbreaking when we read
in the paper or hear on the news how politicians are spending
hundreds of millions of dollars on campaigns to win an election,
or how countries spend billions of dollars on sports events, when
a super star of the big screen, a singer, or a professional sports
player makes millions of dollars for what they do and the poor
teachers, police, and nurses of the world make so little, yet they
are the true heroes of the world; they are the ones making a real
difference everyday in the lives of others and our youth. It is sinful how we glamorize Hollywood stars or politicians and hear
our kids say they are their heroes yet then we hear how they are
arrested for drug use or corruption of their power. These people
have certainly edged God out of their lives and lack the Spirit
to inspire in positive ways or make positive contributions to our
world and society, but it is also not our place to judge anyone.
Each person is in a different place in his or her journey through
life; I do not feel anyone can be judged during the journey, nor
can we judge. That is up to God to do. I have always loved the
parable in Matthew 13:1-23 and Psalm 65 about the seed falling
in different types of ground. The seed that falls on good ground
will produce a fruitful harvest. We can not judge this nor pick
it while it is growing; we must wait. It may have some weeds
among it as it grows; those may be our sins, but in the end, hopefully, the majority of the harvest will be a fruitful one. God does
not want us to judge others not at the beginning of our lives, in
the middle nor even at the end; that is for God to do. We need
to all work toward being the best people we can be while on this

planet. We have to stay focused on what God has in store for each of us in life and live it to the best of our abilities.

We must live a life of goodness and Spirit following God's word; don't worry what others say or do. If we are living by His faith, we have nothing about which to worry. Don't worry about their criticisms; just compete against yourself.

I do feel we should have one world and one dream, but it shouldn't be about sports; competition, whether economic, material, or education, should be about brotherhood and serving one another, letting go and letting God, each of us taking responsibility for ourselves and the planet we all live on and share together, to be honest and kind, to love our fellow humans, to forgive and not to judge others; that is up to God to do. We just need to do our best while on earth, on this school planet moving around the sun. Unfortunately many of today's political leaders (I use this word leaders lightly now, since most so called leaders, I do not feel are true "leaders,") are not like leaders such as Mother Theresa, Gandhi, Martin Luther King, or Francis of Assisi. These so called leaders tend to use their political power to get personal or material gain and power, abusing their authority and not doing the true work of God for "the people" they serve. Just because some one is or has the title of a president, prime minister, chair, senator, director, priest, CEO, superstar or well known sports player doesn't make them "good" or bring true notoriety to them. All of us must earn the respect by our actions and what we do, not just by the title we hold. There are a lot of corrupt police and unfaithful clerics out there not really upholding to their principles or "so called titles." Are they making "positive" contributions to the world? Are they doing what is right and the work for "all" mankind? Like Martin Luther King said, "The ultimate measure of a man is not where he stands in moments of comfort and convenience, but where he stands at times of challenge and controversy." Will you put others' needs in front of your efforts to make more money and run over others? True success is measured by what we can do for others not by all the fame and material goods, money or media notoriety we can gain for ourselves as individuals. Our goal as humans is to conquer evil, not to let evil conquer us. I feel the same about big business and companies too, like big pharmaceutical companies; they often get so much money from grants and external funding to create and discover new vaccines and medicines for illnesses, yet then charge an arm and a leg for the drugs, drugs that cost little to produce, a few cents, yet charging thousands of dollars, making millions of dollars in profits quarterly, going to big CEO's. It seems sinful, to make so much and not give back to humanity. This is ego at work at a larger scale. Sometimes I think that if instead the media (TV, news, Internet, other) would spend more of their energies on working toward resolving world poverty and the grave illnesses that the planet faces instead of putting so much attention to fashion, which politicians are being unfaithful to their spouses, which superstar or NFL player was driving drunk, etc. we could make our world better, more fair for all and might not have the poverty and injustice we have today. It is sad and ironic that some of the so called, "most civilized or developed countries" in the world are the same ones that use their power to start wars, and to kill innocent people and children; they contend to be civilized, high tech, and concerned about human rights, yet interfere with other countries' and cultures' internal affairs, controlling them, telling them how to live and what to do, and if they do not follow suit, threaten them with invasion, wars, and destruction. Is this civilized? Countries can have large egos too; not just individuals.

I have often felt that now living among this world for so many years I now understand why people say things like alcohol, greed, money, and power change everything, and why they are roots to evil; they all seem to be controlled by a devil force when abused or over used and can be hurtful to a society. I guess according to the media, world poverty, AIDS, and genocide are not as glamorous and that is why little attention is brought to them; it is sad that not more is done to address the more important issues in this world, and not the ones related to a politician's infidelity or corruption charges or a superstar's nude photo shoot. For some reason the media feeds these egos of these people and it really is not helping to solve the "real" problems of the world, the ones God wants us to address. God created and formed each one of us the exact way he intended for reasons known to him; he approved of us in our mother's womb. As stated in Jeremiah 1:5, "before I formed you in the womb, I knew and approved of you." God created every one of us on purpose and for a purpose; he knew us before we were born. As Billy Sunday once said, "More people fail from lack of purpose than lack of talent." God approves of each of us; he wants us to live by his word and use our gifts and talents to make positive contributions to this world in which we live. If we were given the gift of knowledge, or ability to make lots of money, or share a disability, or whatever, we need to give this back to others, and share the wealth so to speak; when we live with less ego and more Spirit, we can better share the wealth that God has granted to us with others. Maybe your wealth is the ability to be compassionate or generous; maybe another is the gift of a beautiful voice to sing and share of this in church or in public. As C. H. Spurgeon reminds us, "Your true character is something that no one can injure but yourself."

We need to do more with fewer egos and more Spirit to make this world a better place for all of humanity. We need to live by God's unfolding plan, living by His word, knowing he loves us and he forgives us; his only desire is for us to make him your Lord and Savior. So many in this world are unfortunately too wrapped up in seeking attention of others, making lots of money, having positions of power to control others, and just too consumed by getting and doing more, living without Spirit and hurting others in the process of living. Stop signs are placed on streets for a reason; to prevent injury, we all need law and order to live in a civilized world. Some people want more and more; the more you give them the more they want. They are never happy; money and material things really do not solve the problem, though. I have always loved when I have had pets; they love you unconditionally. They do not care about your money or educational degree, or your Hollywood or NBA fame. They just want to be with you, to share in your company, to pet them, and to love them. We all need to get beyond our egos and think about others, do for others, and to love others. Gandhi once said, "There is enough for every human's need, but not enough for every human's greed." This has become a major problem today; that is why we have so much poverty and inequality in this world. If you want happiness for a lifetime, help others.

Today we also need to be careful of over generalizing about groups of people or by country. Some individuals or groups of people generalize and display their hate with acts of violence and terrorism toward others, generalizing on entire populations like the hate toward Americans in the 911 attacks, the hate toward the Jews during the Holocaust, and the continued hate and discrimination toward gays around the world by many. The Genocide in the Congo and other parts of Africa today is shameful, that we as humans are hurting fellow human beings, even trying to wipe out groups of people. Some terrorists generalize about an entire population by doing evil acts against them; what an ego they must have. What makes them better or gives them more right to think they have the right to do this? No one should ever lose their soul, selling our souls to hate or devilish acts or terrorism. We all need to care enough to do what is right.

Service to others is the key to all success and happiness in life. Search, seek out, develop your faith, and fill your life and world with " The Spirit;" use this faith you've found to reshape the world around you. We need to allow the Spirit in us to help us to turn from sin and keep us on the way that leads to God. God uses us to help turn the lives of others around, to draw all of us closer to our one unique God and source. We must go about to be the hands of God, to scatter joy like seed and all days cherish life, the life He gave us here on earth. When we put God first, live the life he wants us to live; when we put our egos aside and do His will, we will be contributing to our world and lives in positive ways. We will be heroes for ourselves and to God; this should be our only concern, not inflated egos or being better than someone else. No one is truly better than another just because they are rich or white, or famous. A poor uneducated indigenous Indian women has just as much value in God's eyes as any other human here on earth, even if they are from the richest or highest royal family in the world; this doesn't make them better. Money or material goods and fame do not make you better. God promises that the poor and even prostitutes are closer to getting into heaven than the rich and famous. From an old Chinese Proverb, "True wealth is the ability to let go of your possessions;" I agree with this and add to it by saying, "and what you can do for others." We all need to take ego out of the formula of our lives, perhaps considering the following idea in 2 Corinthians 5:15: "Christ died for all, so that living men should not live for themselves, but for Christ who died and was raised to life for them." Don't edge out God; don't let ego destroy your true happiness and our world.

Key Idea from this Chapter:
    Put your ego and self serving ways and attitudes aside. If you want happiness for a lifetime, help others. We are here to serve the world. Use the gifts God gave you to spread those seeds of love and encouragement to others. Share your gifts and wealth, not thinking about what you can get back in return, but how this is going to ultimately make this a better world for all mankind. Service to others is the key to all success and happiness in one's life. A person should measure his or her worth by what he or she can do for others.

Chapter 6
Pray, whether it is Using the Torah, Koran, Bible, Rosary, Prayer Beads, or Yoga, etc.

"Prayer is the best armor we have; it is the key which opens the heart of God."
-Padre Pio of Pietrelcina, Italy

Prayer has been often known as the best medicine. Yet today more and more are moving away from spirituality and religion, stating it doesn't feel right for them or they do not have the time nor interest in religion. Many lose faith in formalized religions when they hear on the news how some contend to be of a particular religion, yet hurt others, take advantage of, or steal from and abuse their parishioners. It is often understandable when many stray away and live without Spirit. We all need to live by our inner light, whether following the Tao Te Ching, Bible, Koran, Torah, ideas from the Buddha, or Hinduism. All cultures have sought out "the Spirit" and have experienced a need for God in their lives and people. Many have seen apparitions of Mother

Joseph M. Furner

Mary or in the past actually spoken to Jesus or Mohammed; everyone has a different degree of faith and varying beliefs depending on their upbringing and interactions in life. One thing we all must do as humans on this earth is we must respect ourselves and each other and take responsibility for our action; we need to live by God's inner light, with Emmanuel, meaning God is in us. We must live the good life of virtue. Whether we are following an inner code of conduct based on the Ten Commandments, a sacred book, or teachings, these principles can be powerful in making our lives more meaningful and happy while protecting our God given planet. In reality, countries, states, and borders from one state or country to another are arbitrary and man made; they only exist on a map or in a person's mind. God never made borders; he wants us to live as one world and one people in harmony with nature, serving others, loving all, judging none, and forgiving all. Human beings themselves created these borders, these lines and maps, these passports and visas, and rights of movement and inequality and injustice, not God. I am convinced we can learn a lot from both good people and bad people; lessons can be learned from both of us too. We are all teachers to others; we are also students. We are one world, and one people. We all need each other for all of us to survive as suggested by the Tao Te Ching over 2500 years ago. The Tao says hidden in all the bad in your life or misfortune, lays the good fortune that will come your way. We must never lose faith. God is good. Goodness will eventually come your way. As we have heard before, a bad man is a good man's job and a good man is a bad man's example. We must all live and use all examples to make the world and ourselves as well as others the best we can be. We must sow seeds of love; we can never sow enough seeds of love in life.

God didn't even want churches or formalized religions which now have become more concerned with money and power than faith. Some churches and religions have become more like sects, attracting people for their money and brainwashing and manipulating them, not to think, but to only accept what the church leaders preach, moving away from God and his "real" message. Some religions have even become so exclusive, that one might not be worthy of even be able to enter into their temples and churches or must get special permission saying they are clean or righteous enough just to do so. Do you think God would approve of this? God is in all of us. God is in me and you, in everyone with whom we interact, of course at varying degree, but he is there. Why on earth would we have to have special permission just to enter a building? Would God like that? Would he be exclusive? He loves us all, he forgives us, he wants us to walk in his way following his teachings, he wants us to make a positive contribution to this world, and care enough to do what is right, he wants us to love others, and he wants us to be kind and accepting.

All religions today have been passed down from many years of history, whether, Catholic, Jewish, Mormon, Muslim, etc. People have certainly influenced the practices and preaching over the years, maybe even perhaps changed things to suit the needs of their ways or beliefs; some feel this happened with the Christian faiths when the Anglicans broke from the Catholic Church due to differences in beliefs about divorce. God did not want formal churches and buildings; this was mentioned in parts of the bible teachings. Instead he wants him in "all" of us, us living by his example of his love for us and our love for one another. If a church is truly a God driven church they would be inclusive of all peoples, sinners, prostitutes, rich and poor, gays, black, women, Catholics and Jews, excepting of all embracing all, encouraging all to come to the fountain and drink of His water. There is no exclusivity to accepting him or being in his presence; there are no special or right prayers we must do to get to him first. Some say the rosary; some, as I saw when I was in Turkey many years ago, believe that carrying prayer beads and repeating all the ways to say God on the beads is the way. Prayer can be chants, it can be silence, and it may be formal or informal. It is a way we can connect to our "Spirit or source" and live out his wishes for us here on earth. Prayer may involve Yoga and special breathing techniques; what ever way you use to connect to our source, our God, we must know that there is no one right way. Prayer is not just asking for help or "things;" I like the idea about which the Dalai Lama speaks, living a life respecting yourself, others, being responsible for all your actions and being gentle with the Earth. Sometimes not getting what we want can be a wonderful stroke of luck. God knows exactly what each of us needs at all times. Thank him, love him, and know it is his will; we are all put on this Earth for a purpose, the main purpose is to serve and love each other, to love your neighbor as yourself. If you still have a pulse, then you still have a purpose in life. Use it to serve God and others.

Prayer is speaking to Yahweh or God. To some it also may mean speaking and praying to other saints or holy leaders, using them as intermediaries to our God, like St. Jude or Mother Mary. People can pray together or alone. It can be formal or informal. It can be using prayer books and formal prayers or speaking adlib personally to your source within you. Based on the teachings of St. Anthony of Padua and others, I think there are different parts to and types of prayer. Prayer is often a quiet personal endeavor when we connect to our God. It can also be a plea for help, support, and for goods which are temporary that we find necessary for our earthly life here. Prayer is important and it is okay to ask and plea for His support, but we must always remember that Adonai or God knows what one really needs in life and what is best; we need to always remember it is always "His will." If we do not always get what we want or pray for, God will provide you with something even better, something much grander than you even expected often times. Sometimes we can pray and pray asking of so much and then when it doesn't come, we are let down. We need to know that God knows exactly what one needs. Instead of petitioning for requests and favors, instead say we need to pray that "God will bless us with His will." I also like to say, "Lord, make me more like you." One aspect of prayer that I feel many of us as humans forget about is of "thanksgiving." Not only do we need to pray for ourselves and others and our needs, but we need to give thanks to God for all he has bestowed on us in our lives; we need to thank him for all his blessings, favors, and abundance in our lives, things like a good family and upbringing, an education, a good job, a nice place to live, etc. There are many blessings we receive daily, even whether one may not think so; an illness can also often be a blessing in disguise. We may need the rest or wake up call to change our lives a certain way.

Prayer and having faith are so important, God is good and we must always remember this. Albert Einstein in his book titled *God vs. Science* in 1921 said, "Evil does not exist, or at least it does not exist unto itself. Evil is simply the absence of God. It is just like darkness and cold, a word that man has created to describe the absence of God. God did not create evil. Evil is the result of

Joseph M. Furner

what happens when man does not have God's love present in his heart. It's like the cold that comes when there is no heat or the darkness that comes when there is no light." We see it everyday, it is in the daily example of man's inhumanity to man. It is in the multitude of crime and violence everywhere in the world. These manifestations are nothing else but evil, but they are caused by man's lack of faith and lack of Spirit, an absence of God. This is why prayer and living in Spirit are so critical to living well.

God wants to give us his blessings. All we need to do is ask him for them. We often need to close the door to the noise of exterior things whether it is literal noise, or the pressures for material goods, money, power, and overall competition in this world; detach yourselves and your preoccupations from earthly things. Praying and connecting to God daily is healthy; we need to feel his Spirit in us and live our lives knowing we are doing his will for the betterment of the planet and others. Not only is prayer asking for help or giving thanks, it is also listening to God; we need to ask him to speak to us, telling us internally what and how we should be living our lives, how we should handle situations, what we should do, and how we should behave. God sends us so many messages in our lifetime; it may be in our inner voice, or it may be through other people. Some may contend they can be our angels; it may be through both positive and negative experiences, but he is sending us messages. We need to open our hearts to hear him and feel his message, and connect to the Spirit; it is in us and all about us. Reading the Bible, Koran, Torah, Tao Te Ching and other holy scripture can also bring us closer to the Spirit. While some readings may be hard to understand and follow, some have parables and messages; the holy books all offer us solace and guidance to live a better sound life based on

36

principles grounded in our God, our one God we all worship. We are all sons and daughters of Abraham on this earth; we are brothers and sisters. We need each other, we need to pray for each other, and we need to pray for the best world we can have. Who knows, maybe we can have heaven here on earth if we live by his ways loving one another? I really do feel that prayer is the key to the heart of God. Ourselves, others, and the world as a whole can never have enough prayers or positive vibes being sent our way; prayer is critical. We all need to pray more. Oswald Chambers once said, "When a person is at his wits' end, it is not a cowardly thing to pray. It is the only way to get into touch with reality." As Evelyn Heinz once wrote, "Daily prayer brings peace." Prayer is critical. Pray, pray, pray!

Key Idea from this Chapter:

Prayer comes in many forms. We may pray together or alone. We may use formal prayer recitations or speak to God informally. We may pray for things or cures, but we need to know, though, that God knows what is best for us and it is always His will. Prayer should include giving thanks for blessings received. There is not just one right religion or prayer. We need to listen to God, connect with him, and ask him to speak to us; we need to listen as a part of prayer as well. We need to live by God's way; we need to pray to God for ourselves and others. Prayer is the key to connecting to our Spirit. Prayer brings solace and contentment to our lives and world. We cannot shine if we have not taken the time to fill our lamps; prayer is the way to do this.

Chapter 7

Have High Standards, Strive for the Best, Don't Settle for Mediocrity

"Don't settle for anything less than God's best."
-Joel Osteen

I hear many people complain today that when they go to a store, office, or public place and interact with the public or service people, let's say for example if we were renewing our driver's license, we are confronted with people who do not seem to care about us or who we are as people, the public. Today's world has become a fast-paced out of control place where everyone is rushing to "do do do," but so many of us are doing things in a mediocre manner; we leave church before the mass is officially over, we short change our children by putting more emphasis on sports than academics, and we allow our government to do a poor job in protecting us or providing services to the needy and its citizens. Mediocrity seems to reign supreme in today's world. So many are so much more concerned in having "more" than in having "quality." When is this madness going to stop? It is going to stop when each one of us stops letting our country, government, and others control us and silence us. It is also going to stop when we all decide as individuals to live by the laws of God and do the "right" things by ourselves, others, and our Mother Earth. When we stop letting others make us feel we need to conform to consumerism and just an acceptable way of "living." We must all decide that we are going to live "righteously" doing what is right by ourselves and our co-world citizens and our mother earth. We all must care enough to do what is right and work toward living and leaving a legacy of quality for our God and others, but more importantly for ourselves, as we deserve it; it is our reputations at stake. We can no longer settle for living lives of mediocrity; others, mankind as a whole, and our mother earth will suffer if we do.

Martin Luther King Jr. didn't do it alone either for the entire African-American community; they united and worked toward equal rights and the appropriate attention as peacefully as they could. While many were being lynched and persecuted, they persevered until justice was actuated. Just as gays are now trying to do and will achieve some day very soon. The greed, corruption, incompetence, insecurities, power-trips, and big egos are destructive to all people and our world. The elected officials from around the world are here to serve us, the people; they are supposed to be listening and looking out for us, not giving in and selling out our cities, states, and countries to big business and developers. It is sad when many of our current elected officials try to silence people, when they talk down to us in a condescending way, or accuse them of lying or fabricating the "truth," when they do not allow people to speak, and try to control all as leaders instead of listening to their constituents and governing based on their wishes. When managers, directors, and others in businesses or positions of power won't respond to e-mails, com-plaints, concerns, or poor service; instead they are sarcastic and give an attitude to the ones they are hired to serve. It is sad when some police or police chief or other leaders refuses to step down although they can't do the job and get a handle on the crime or problems in an institution. Ineffective leaders and incompetence is a problem in the 21st Century, and because "we care" and speak out we are made to feel bad. We need to get all people involved, all people to vote, and all people to make decisions not to shop or frequent places that do not respect their people. We need to have a government we can trust and feel they listen to us and vote/make decisions based on us "the people." Too many seem self serving and are not representing our wishes as the people in this world.

I understand why I hear and read about so many people now that are losing faith in their governments, and considering why we are not able to trust them. The people need to vote out any poor leaders who do not respect us and are not doing their jobs. We need to continue speaking out, with editorials, letters, phone calls, by attending meetings, visits during leaders' office hours, and requesting to speak to the person in charge. We all deserve better and should not let today's leaders silence us; do not let them prohibit you from having a voice. You matter; we all matter. Mother Earth matters; we must never give up against mediocrity. We have to be better than those who do not take a stand on the poor quality of life of others. WE MUST PEACE-FULLY WORK TOWARD A "CARING COMMUNITY." A caring community is one where leaders listen and care; where they are effective, transparent, and accountable. We all want peace here; we need to work for that and not allow this medi-

Joseph M. Furner

ocrity. God bless the caring citizens who are willing to step up and speak out against mediocrity. We must never settle for less than the best; that is what God wants us to do. We shouldn't be content with being average. Average is as close to the bottom as it is to the top. As Vince Lombardi once said, "The quality of a person's life is in direct proportion to their commitment to excellence, regardless of their chosen field of endeavor."

A story in the Koran (or Quran) that a friend told me about has to do with the prophet Joseph (or Yusuf). In the Quran, there is a chapter on Yusuf in Chapter 12: Verse 4. "When Yusuf said to his father: O my father! surely I saw eleven stars and the sun and the moon—I saw them making obeisance to me....Yusufali: (but the treaties are) not dissolved with those pagans with whom ye have entered into alliance and who have not subsequently failed you in aught, nor aided any one against you. So fulfill your engagements with them to the end of their term: for Allah loveth the righteous. Pickthal: excepting those of the idolaters with whom ye (Muslims) have a treaty, and who have since abated nothing of your right nor have supported anyone against you. (As for these), fulfill their treaty to them till their term. Lo! Allah loveth those who keep their duty (unto him). Shakir: except those of the idolaters with whom you made an agreement, then they have not failed you in anything and have not backed up any one against you, so fulfill their agreement to the end of their term; surely Allah loves those who are careful (of their duty)." The idea of keeping one's word and following through are important messages here, as our the ideas of having an allegiance, as God or Allah wants us to keep our word and stick it out to the end, and to do the very best we can, always, with everything we do.

Volunteering in our world and community is another way to work toward not accepting mediocrity and improving our world as a whole. I personally think volunteering is very important and rewarding. If we are going to live in a community or county, we should volunteer where we can, and if we can, to make it better. I realize some have more time than others depending on where they are in their career and lifestyle, other commitments, etc. Volunteering is rewarding and allows you to have a direct impact on your community and quality of life. If we didn't care, we wouldn't speak out or volunteer. Many of us do care, so we are involved; this is what I think God wants us to do. Many citizens in countries go to city commission meetings, neighborhood meetings, we may volunteer at crime walks, and do lot clean ups, neighborhood yard sales, and help with elections and other civic events. It is great to be able to serve on committees, both locally and nationally, or internationally; we should be involved as world citizens. A few years ago I was on an adhoc code enforcement board; it was rewarding to have a say about and input into making things better where I live. I do volunteer work at the senior center in my area and work with many Cubans who speak only Spanish there; I have done it for about 13 years now. I have volunteered at my church, bringing a lady shopping, to the doctor's, to mass or getting her groceries. I work with a local school here in Lake Worth as well and have for many years now. I also serve on several national and international editorial boards as part of my work. I agree; volunteering is so rewarding. Not only am I helping others, but it also makes me feel good knowing I am involved and contributing to society in a positive way. I think God put all of us here on Earth to serve; volunteering is one way to serve and impact your world in a positive way. I wish our elected leaders would do all their work as a mayor/

commissioner/governor/president without pay like I do; it might make them more honest and more likely to truly support their constituents in an honest manner. They are paid for what they do; when we volunteer, we are not. That is what makes the difference. Someday I would consider doing that but without pay; for now, with my job/career, spouse in a foreign country and having to travel a lot, and other issues, I cannot assume a role like mayor or president at this time in my career, but I will continue to do as much volunteer work as I can do to try to make positive contributions to my city, community, and world. As Thomas Jefferson once said, "In matters of style, swim with the current: in matters of principle, stand like a rock." I think this is so true. We need our leaders to behave this way as they lead and represent us all. We can be good role models by respecting our laws, participating all we can, keeping our properties up, and respecting our fellow human beings. I think volunteering does bring a bit of solace and peace to your life; it makes you feel good by helping others. It is a major step away from mediocrity in our world now. I have always felt the way one should look at how one measures success in life is by what they can do for others. It is not about material or monetary gain. True wealth is the ability to let go of your possessions and serve others. When we help others, we are also helping ourselves and ultimately humanity as a whole.

I know many people and communities use petitions to impact change and work toward improvements. People get fed up with the status quo or mediocrity in the world so they all join forces and sign petitions with the hope that change will come about. From experience, petitions don't always seem to work in all communities or institutions, but we as world citizens need to peacefully work toward change, for improvements and for not having mediocrity in our communities and world. Blight and crime are problems with which many communities and countries are dealing today and our leaders do very little about it. Blight seems to be taking a strong hold all over and some people seem to think it is their right to contribute to it. The slumlords are growing around the world, buying up cheap properties, renting them out at high costs, yet not taking care of their properties. It is a problem all over; often these same slumlords are the same people who are rich and own the big development companies and give kickbacks to political leaders to look the other way until they are ready to finally develop an area. Many areas now have extremely high rental rates and still major overcrowding exists all over; the quality of living for many people is declining and standards seem to be slipping, especially for middle and low income (poor) people. The rich keep getting richer and the poor poorer with a worsening quality of life. I know of some houses where I live that have up to 20 guys living in a small two bedroom one bathroom house; it's no wonder they are all hanging around outside and urinating in their hedges. In my community, I applaud the compassion of one of the city's elected commissioners; she is a real advocate for the poor and for illegal immigrants, but if she really wants to raise the standard for them and all people in the community, she must make sure our codes, people, and city are upholding all of our laws and enforcing them for all residences; she is not really helping the illegal immigrants by not allowing them to live to the same high standard by which we all want to live here in our community. Like my friend from México, Juan, said to me, we are in another country, the USA; we must abide by the laws and codes here, and not like it was in our country if we want to be here. We cannot keep allowing forms of lawlessness; it only perpetuates more lawlessness. I actually feel sorry for the

Joseph M. Furner

illegal immigrants here; whether many realize it or not most are humans trafficked here, having to pay upward of $5000 or more to come to the USA. They are promised a wonderful life and lots of money. They now are deceived; most now cannot get work and it is harder and harder for them. They are our modern day slaves for many Americans, mostly big business; it is sad. The employers reap the benefits of their cheap labor; it almost seems as if it is a hidden government agenda to have them here, and that is why the laws are overlooked as it relates to them here in this city and in the USA—-it is likely all about "Development." There is always a price to pay for mediocrity; some pay more than others. We must do more; we must be kind to all people. We must pray for them, ourselves, and our leaders so that we can have high standards for all people. Maybe having the "Americas" united where we can all live and work legally in any of the Americas is the way, but we need to do it legally; we need to stop human trafficking of the illegal immigrants. We need to have higher standards for them, and we must make all feel as equal parts, paying their fair share of taxes and abiding by all the same laws we have here. Until we address the illegal immigrants and have high standards for their living, I do not think we are going to get rid of the blight, crime, and all the social ills that plague the USA, and also many other parts of the world as well. Our elected leaders do very little at all levels and perhaps the one thing we can do is pray to find some solace to the problem.

Like Buckminster Fuller once said, *"Everyone is born a genius, but the process of living de-geniuses them."* When we live with such egos, hurting and taking advantage of others, when we settle for mediocrity and a low standard of living and doing things, we only bring all of us down. We all need to lift "all" of us up by

46

all being equal, listening, doing our very best, living by law and order, following the "Spirit," and living by His suggested ways.

A favorite passage from the Torah that a friend told me about is Mishna 14. The Mishnas are the fundamental works of Jewish Oral Law. They are the ethical and moral statements of the Talmudical Sages. "He (Hillel) used to say, if I am not for me who is for me, if I am for myself what am I, and if not now when." Hillel begins by saying no one other than myself can "be for me." The idea is that the inspiration required to face life cannot come from without. No one else can turn us on; no one can give us the zeal to live up to life's challenges. Our teachers, parents, etc. may momentarily startle us into proper behavior but it will be transient. The only way to truly accomplish in life and achieve our goals is to feel that sense of excitement and fulfillment about growing into life's challenges. We must know what our goals are, and 'we' must want to realize them. Hillel continues, "If I am for myself, what am I." This means that even if I do inspire myself and accomplish goals, I am not wholly worthy. My accomplishments can always be greater. We need to focus and direct our energies towards ourselves. However, we should not become exclusively engrossed in ourselves and our own development. Ultimately, our interests are in improving mankind. Each of us might focus primarily on him- or herself, but this is not to imply we are unconcerned with the rest of mankind. We must never lose site of our cosmic mission to the world. Although we are for ourselves, that is because we are truly for all mankind. Finally, Hillel concludes, "if not now when." We all have our inspired moments in life. We reach emotional highs, perhaps while hearing a stirring piece of music, during intense conversation, or in those special moments in which we sense something has

Joseph M. Furner

touched our lives. We cannot let those moments pass. On the one hand, of course they will; inspiration is by nature fleeting and transient. Yet we must hold onto them. How so? We can do this by concretizing the moment. Decide to become a better person. Make some small but tangible improvement in your life. Make it whatever you see as your personal challenge or next step at that moment in your life. However, whatever it is, make sure it's something real and concrete. This personal challenge might be learning another language, or it might be getting an education, whether high school or college. We need to do things for ourselves that can help us to then make positive contributions to the world. If we don't, yet another inspired moment of life will be lost forever. We cannot live with constant inspiration, but we can build upon those fleeting yet precious moments of true awareness. Ultimately, we will learn to be for ourselves—and so for all mankind. For if not now, when? I think this is all so true; it is something to consider as each person works on impacting his/her own life and the world, no holding back, not settling for mediocrity, take chances, and knowing if you do not do it, then who will? We sometimes have to just have a "just do it attitude"; we need to do it as others might not and it may make the world a better place. Like Eleanor Roosevelt once said: "The future belongs to those who believe in the beauty of their dreams." I think this is so true; we must have dreams. We must have accomplishments; we all must dream and do things for ourselves and others, and we must do it all with the highest standard possible we can to live a legacy of honor, of high honor, for our God and world.

Key Idea from this Chapter:

Do not settle for mediocrity in your life. Improve yourself, by getting a good education, living a righteous life, keeping the "Spirit" in you, and making positive contributions to the world.

Get involved; speak out; volunteer; run for an elected office; attend meetings; be involved and have a "just do it attitude;" and sign petitions; never be silenced though in working toward making a better world for all of humankind. Don't settle for anything less than God's best in all you do and live in your life. Be the example you want all others to live by.

Chapter 8

Live Life, Read Books, Watch Movies and TV, Some of the Best Movies, Books and TV to Lift your Spirit

"The man who does not read good books has no advantage over the man who can't read."
-Mark Twain

We have to live our lives; we do this by the people we encounter in life, but we also do it by other ways we interact with people and the people we see in movies, TV, and in stories and books we might read. We have to care enough though about what we and our families read and watch. There are many great resources out there that we can use to help us find life, joy, and sadness in the lives of others. While we should find our own joy in life, we can do this too by reading, watching TV, going to the movies, and even listening to music. I once heard someone

Joseph M. Furner

say that "the best art is created under oppression." I think this is true. Sometimes some of the best literature out there was written and inspired by actual events, of sad events, or due to oppression. It is often sad, but very true. I like when the literature is then turned into movies on the big screen, movies like *Schindler's List* as an example, it is so sad and it breaks your heart to see what really happened as part of our humanity here on earth, the killing of innocent people due to their religious beliefs, but there was some good that came out of it too, with many people saved thanks to Mr. Schindler and his efforts. Literature, movies, and even TV can inspire, teach, and sometimes even lighten up the burdens of everyday life by connecting to the people as they see things come to light in the reality of our own lives. St. Teresa of Avila believed that God speaks to us and calls on us in many ways. His appeals come through the conversations of good people, or from sermons, or through the reading of "good books;" and there are many other ways, of which you have heard, in which God calls us. They can even come through sicknesses and trials, or by means of truths which God teaches us at times when we are engaged in prayer, meditation, concentration, or interacting with other humans. So, through books, movies, music, and even TV, sometimes God's message is sent out to us; we need to be opened to listening for it at all times.

Besides reading the Bible, Koran, Torah, Tao Te Ching or other "spiritual" holy books, reading and entertaining ourselves is important and part of our everyday lives in today's modern world. Helen Keller once said, "From your parents you learn love and laughter and how to put one foot in front of the other. But when books are opened, you discover that you have wings." Today it seems more people watch more TV than read books. Many humans are in front of the TV or computer daily for hours, looking to find out information about what is going on in the world through watching news and information channels. We watch sitcoms and reality shows; we seek out the media to relax, to connect, and to unwind. We look at *Facebook* and *Myspace* for hours on the computer. Sometimes reading, watching TV, or going to the movies is healthy and pleasurable; these activities are useful for self-improvement as well. While I do not advocate sitting in front of the TV for hours watching the news, which can often become too negative and one sided, I do think we all need to be informed as world citizens. Too, it may not always be healthy to watch TV or movies that only emphasize violence, materialism, vulgarity, and sex. We all need to error on the side of caution and read reviews of books, TV shows and movies and be sure to see that they have an element of meaning and depth to them that can help us grow, become better people, and care about our fellow humans and our Mother Earth. We need to care enough to watch what we allow into our temples (or our bodies and souls); some of the material out there now is too violent, too vulgar, and shows too much sex and consumerism. It is not healthy to desensitize ourselves to this type of living, especially for children and young people. I personally think that the *Public Broadcasting Station* (PBS), without commercials and funded by the viewers, is likely more wholesome and informative to watch than much of the mainstream TV channels and cable. Too, I am not saying we need to replace the TV, a book, or movies for family activities and outings; they all have a place in life and to be plopped down in front of a TV, book, movie screen, or computer instead of spending quality time with your family and loved ones doing other engaging activities, such as going to church, attending a sporting event, playing miniature golf, swimming, horseback ridding, etc., which are often more meaningful and fulfilling in the long run. You are creating positive memories with your family. These are all important bonding moments as well. We do, though, need to face the fact that TV and the media do play a big part of our lives, so, we need to watch things that are going to make us laugh or be informed, to see the purpose of life, and to live life to the fullest. I have compiled a list of suggested books, movies, and TV shows (some which you may want to buy on DVD now) which can help to address family values, where we can laugh as a family, and where we can grow together, making this world a better place for all people.

Movies

Pay it Forward—this is a great movie about an experiment to pass on good deeds to others; when someone does something nice or good, you must then do it to a few people as well. This movie is so inspirational, it makes you want to be part of this world, do good, and be a good example, passing on love and kindness.

To Kill a Mockingbird—is a great movie and book which shows how a single father teaches his children about integrity by his own example. We all must strive to live lives that have integrity and values.

Red Sky at Morning—the movie shows how difficult it is to be yourself amid peer pressure and the trials and tribulations of personal development, with which all of us as humans struggle. We all experience peer pressure, especially young people; we are all trying to fit in.

Living Well: Caring Enough To Do What's Right

Stand and Deliver—is a powerful movie about a teacher believing in his students and knowing they can do it. It is about values, love, and hard work. Teachers play such an instrumental role in the lives of our young people and often go unrecognized. This is an inspirational story of success for students who were at risk.

While there are millions of excellent movies out there to watch, these are just a few really good ones. Research and read reviews, be inspired by stories of love, integrity, honesty, values, caring teachers, and challenges to make a true difference in this world. I heard once that the best way to stop kids from seeing R- and X-rated movies is to label them "educational." We need to watch meaningful material, material that is going to touch our Spirit.

TV Shows (Old and New)

Friends—funny, right from wrong, modern day occurrences, and nice chance to laugh and share with friends and families.

The Brady Bunch—an old favorite from the 70's, with so many great family values and story lines; every family will certainly connect to the episodes.

Little House on the Prairie—this is a great old T.V. show from the 70's and early 80's, based on books from Laura Ingalls Wilder. It is a great family TV show about values, being raised during agrarian times, and the responsibilities of each family member. A must-see, buy the DVD series; your family will love it. This is one of my all time favorites.

The Walton's—another classic from the 1970's about a large nuclear family growing up in the south dealing with issues of hard times during the depression. The Walton family is a family united helping each other and learning proper values. This is another must-have series.

Touched by an Angel—-is another great show from the 1990's that touched the hearts of many. Every episode made you cry and showed you God in ordinary people and circumstances. Love lives on in this great show.

The Nanny—a more recent TV sitcom that is still being shown occasionally with Fran Drescher. This is a really funny show about a nanny working for a wealthy playwright, and who is helping to raise his three children. It is a comedy with some really good laughs and values as well.

I Love Lucy—a classic with Lucille Ball. This is true comedy that still makes you laugh today. We all need to laugh; this show will certainly do this.

Joel Osteen—a great half-hour Trinity Broadcasting Network show is another form of church to tune into each week. Joel really connects to the audience, bringing hope, love, and inspiration to all people, teaching you that God loves you and wants the very best for you. This is one of my current weekly favorites.

There are many wonderful TV shows past, present, and current. For example, *The Office* is known for its unusual comedy and narratives. We need to have balance in our lives and a little TV, laughter, love, values, and human tenderness are essential.

Overdoing it may not be healthy, but a little is not hurtful. We all need a little diversion from daily living. I once heard that as an educational device, TV rates above everything else. No nation in history has ever known as much as we do now about detergents and deodorants.

Books

Interior Castle by St. Teresa of Avila is a profound book about spirituality. St. Teresa is one of the first women Doctors of the Catholic Church. Her book is the most celebrated book on mystical theology in existence. Her writing was to guide souls toward spiritual perfection, spiritual knowledge, humility, and balance in life.

The Aladdin Factor by Jack Canfield is a great resource for personal development and growth. He is also an author of the *Chicken Soup for the Soul* series which has inspirational true stories that will touch your soul.

Tuesdays with Morie by Mitch Albom, a sad true story about a professor who is dying. This book is filled with stories of love, life, and hope. It is a great book from which we can learn that we all have a purpose in life.

The Night Before Christmas by Clement Clark Moore is a classic Christmas story/poem of hope for children with rhyming surprises. Children and adults alike will love this one.

Angela's Ashes by Frank McCourt is a great story of an Irish family growing up in poverty which shows family values as well as their trials and tribulations. Sometimes reality hurts; we all need to remember from where we came.

All you Really need to know about Prayer you can Learn from the Poor by Louise Perrotta is a wonderful set of stories from people who are poor or work with the poor in some of the poorest Caribbean nations. The stories will touch your life and give you hope that there really is a God working in all of us; the stories show us how powerful prayer really can be.

The Power of Intention by Wayne Dyer is an excellent self-help book that will help you connect to God and be intentional in all you do. Realizing your full potential, you can make a difference in your life, the lives of others, and the world around you.

There are thousands of books written today that can touch your heart. Taking the time to read is a gift God has given us. Each of us has a book within us that needs to be written as well; consider that the next time you read a book. Think about what story you can tell. Whether fiction or non-fiction, science-fiction, etc., each person has his/her own genre or interest; we need to encourage others to read and learn from others, to see other points of view and ideas, to have our minds expanded, and to grow. While life is about balance and we cannot always have our heads in a book, books do bring us much wisdom; however, based on a quote from John Wesley, "Beware you be not swallowed up in books! An ounce of love is worth a pound of wisdom," we need to do all with balance whether it is reading, watching TV, or going to the movies. I do think, though, that reading is a powerful tool; we can learn so much from a book. I once heard someone say, "Those who don't read have no advantage over those who can't." Take a look; it is in a book. Open one up and "just read."

We need to always be open when we read, watch TV, go to see a movie, and even listen to music to see God at work teaching us lessons in life; sending certain people our way, He works in mysterious ways. While I mostly emphasized books, TV, and movies here, I think music is also a way for us to get closer to God and learn to do what is right. I enjoy listening to the radio, particularly the local contemporary Christian rock channel, which, in my case, is 88.1WAY FM; I find the music uplifting, giving me a positive outlook on life, bringing me closer to God, and acting out what he wishes for me. I also think a lot of the classical music today is also very inspirational, whether one likes Bach, Beethoven, Vivaldi, or even soothing piano music by George Winston, who is more contemporary; this type of music can touch the soul in a special way. Around the Christmas holidays, I particularly like the *Messiah* by Handel; *For unto us a Child is Born* is a song that just lifts you on high. We all need to be aware of how God is working through the media to touch our lives, to help us to be good people, and do what is right in this world.

Key Idea from this Chapter:

Realize that we must have balance in our lives. A little bit of TV is healthy and a diversion for us in our daily lives. We need to seek out material that makes us laugh, teaches us values, and perhaps connects us with Spirit. Too much TV or news can be negative and can desensitize you to the ills of this world; we need to be careful and have balance. Listening to music, reading, and watching movies are other ways to learn and grow, to teach us

Joseph M. Furner

values and integrity. We cannot escape from the material world in which we now live, but we can learn a lot to not become so involved in this consumerism and learn the real important values in life through stories, music, and movies that can touch your heart and make you and this world a better place in which to live.

Chapter 9

The 10 Commandments-Keep Focused on God and Heaven—Don't get Consumed by this Earth, Materialism, and Competition, etc.

"This is my commandment, that you love one another as I have loved you."
-Jesus.

We need to always remember, Emmanuel, meaning, "God is with us." Anything we do to the least of our brothers we do unto him; God is in all of us. We must live our lives with rectitude. I think the Ten Commandments are the best rules of life for all human beings to follow and all religions as well; if we all followed and respected the commandments, we would likely have a lot of peace in this world. God is with us; he made sure he was in all of us. It is a small bit compared to the offering he made on Calvary for our sins.

No matter what religion, we have all heard of the Ten Commandments; as many know, they are a list of religious and moral imperatives that, according to Judeo-Christian tradition, were written by God and given to Moses on Mount Sinai in the form of two stone tablets (Exodus 20:2-17 and Deuteronomy 5:6-21). The Ten Commandments are often known as an ethical or ritual Decalogue for all human beings (earthlings) by which to live. Various religions divide these statements among the Commandments in different ways, and may also translate the Commandments differently. In my opinion, they are good rules for all of us to live by so that we all interact and live together in a world made up of many people, all of whom are diverse yet, at the same time, have many things in common. If all people lived by these rules, perhaps we would have heaven here on earth, with all of us interacting with each other, respecting one another, and cooperating in a way that allows all of us to live here peacefully. We all need to remember that when someone does you wrong, don't do what comes naturally; do what comes supernaturally. Love him.

The Ten Commandments are as follows:

1. I am the Lord your God, you shall not have strange Gods before me.

2. You shall not take the name of the Lord your God in vain.

3. Remember the Sabbath day and keep it holy.

4. Honor your father and your mother, so that your days may be long in the land that the Lord your God is giving you.

5. You shall not murder.

6. You shall not commit adultery.

7. You shall not steal.

8. You shall not bear false witness against your neighbor.

9. You shall not covet your neighbor's wife.

10. You shall not covet your neighbor's belongings.

Today, we live in a world in which many live vengefully, wanting to get back at their offenders and have an "eye for an eye mentality," sometimes known as the "Eye for an eye, tooth for a tooth" or the code of the Pashtuns (Matthew 5:38). This set of rules is also called the Code of Hammurabi. Hammurabi was King of Babylon, from 1792-1750 BC. The code survives today in the Akkadian language and it also shows up in Deuteronomy 19:21: *"Thus you shall not show pity: life for life, eye for eye, tooth for tooth, hand for hand, foot for foot.* It also shows up in Matthew 5:21: *"You have heard that the ancients were told, 'YOU SHALL NOT COMMIT MURDER ' and 'Whoever commits murder shall be liable to the court.'* Well, perhaps we all need to know that the court is God; He will return to address such acts. As human beings we must protect others from being harmed, and may need to incarcerate violators or ones who put others in danger; perhaps it really is God who should be the one to have final judgment on one's life, not human beings, by killing them for taking the lives of others. This is something for all of us to think about; it just doesn't make logical sense. I do not see the logic in the notion that for every wrong done there should be a compensating measure of justice. Instead, we need to honor the Ten Commandments, and try to have everyone do what God has commanded us to do. We should not always focus so much on what people are doing wrong, but on what people are doing right. The "eye for an eye, and a tooth for a tooth" mentality is not logical; it does not follow our God's rules and teachings of love, forgiveness, and repentance. When you read various sections in the Holy books about this, it is all up for interpretation; it really almost sounds like it is saying the direct opposite of doing this. A more Christian view is two wrongs do not make a right. I really believe that an evil act can't be corrected with more evil. Like Jesus, Gandhi and Martin Luther King proved, we as humans can accomplish much more through peaceful means. Two wrongs don't make a right. Some people believe that responding to evil with evil is a major indicator of a person who believes in materialism. I feel that "two wrongs make a right" is a logical fallacy that occurs when it is assumed that if one wrong is committed, another wrong will cancel it out. Like many fallacies, it typically appears as the hidden major premise in an enthymeme—an unstated assumption which must be true for the premises to lead to the conclusion. Like in mathematics/geometry this is an example of an informal fallacy. We all must think about this carefully and think about the fact that if all of us as humans are going to live our lives using this flawed logic, then we are only hurting ourselves.

Like St. Theresa of Avila believed, we cannot put out fire with more fire, for revenge is not forgiving; we must give second chances. We must not be the court; God is the court. God will return to judge the living and the dead. Love your God and know that our God will fight our battles for us; he will prevail with the justice that is right. Many countries, like mine, the USA, allow for the death penalty; it sets a very bad precedent for "human rights." The belief that since a person murdered a person, he or she shall be murdered employs a flawed logic. No wonder the USA has the highest murder rates in the world. Murder is murder whether it is a person acting this way toward another human being or if it is a government doing it toward a person because they killed someone. We as a people must be better than this one person or this government; we must do what is "right," and not murder as stated in the Ten Commandments. If we do what that one person did, and then we are no better than the original murderer. Murder is wrong; there is nothing right about killing another human being, not for war, not for removing someone from power, not for ego reasons, or anything. Murder is unacceptable, and as humans we are being told not to do it, not as individuals or as a government; we may need to address a situation, incarcerate or imprison for the protection of the masses, but killing is unacceptable. I like how Jesus said, "If you slap my right cheek, I will turn my face for you to slap my left as well." Jesus is the forgiving grace we have all been giving on earth; to act against our rules from God, to use flawed logic by humans and bad interpretations just plain doesn't make sense. We all must be loving and forgiving, giving others always another chance to repent and change their ways. We are not the court; let's leave that up for our God, our Allah. As Galatians 6:7 reminds us, "Don't be misled-you cannot mock the justice of God. You will always harvest what you plant." I once read that there is growing evidence of the beneficial relationship between communities and high church attendance. I heard that the city with the highest church attendance in the USA is Provo, UT; it is also recognized to have one of the lowest crime rates in the nation. Inversely, crime is rampant in some areas where church attendance is very low. When people and neighborhoods have faith communities, when they care enough to do what is right, when they abide by laws and commandments, when they care about themselves and others, crime in their communities is less and a sense of Spirit lives in their midst. James Allen once said, "Work joyfully and peacefully, knowing that right thoughts and right efforts will inevitably bring about right results." We all need to do this if we are going to achieve harmony in our world and in our own individual beings.

One of my favorite passages comes from the *Book of Common Prayer*; the passage is used in most Episcopal Churches as follows:

> "Thou shalt love the Lord thy God with all thy heart, and with all thy soul, and with all thy mind. This is the first and great commandment. And the second is like unto it: Thy shalt love thy neighbor as thyself. On these two commandments hang all the law and the prophet." Matthew 22: 37-40.

This idea is so profound, that we as humans need to learn to love our neighbors as ourselves. What a wonderful concept and I am sure an even better world it would be if we could all love one another as ourselves. The Catholic Church also has a prayer called the "Act of Love," which is similar and should also be part of all humans' mission statement in life as follows:

> "O my God, I love You above all things, with my whole heart and soul, because You are all-good and worthy of all love. I love my neighbor as myself for the love of You. I forgive all who have injured me and ask pardon of all who I have injured."

The idea of loving God, ourselves, and our neighbors, forgiving each other's offenses is so beautiful; it is what our God wants us to do. They likely are the most basic rules and most important commandments one could live by in life. What a wonderful world it would be if we could all live by this example. We need to pave our way to a new humanity, to unite, and care enough to do what is right for all humanity. It all comes back to what Jesus said, "This is my commandment, that you love one another as I have loved you." This is likely the most important lesson God wants us to learn and practice in life, a life of living well.

Key Idea from this Chapter:

Get yourself to say prayers, live by the rules of your good faith, and to practice this in all you do in life. Be kind to others, do what is right, forgive, and sin less. Know that we all may have been given a cross to bear in life, God has a purpose set out for you; find it and complete this mission in an upright, ethical way. Don't allow this world, which is not our world, to consume you with materialism or name brands, and to consume us to sin and hurt others in the process. We need to abide by laws of the community and faith to create a world of love. Love the Lord, love yourself, and love your neighbor.

❧

Chapter 10
The Living Well Prayer

But as for me and my house, we will serve the Lord.
- Joshua 24:15

I firmly believe that a person is living well when they are in Spirit. A person is also at peace and knows right from wrong. Often times it is helpful to pray daily to bring us back to our Source. Prayer, meditation, and positive living help us connect to our Creator which in return fills us with peace. *The Living Well Prayer* is simple; you can memorize it within a few short times of saying it and you can also alter it to suit your style and needs. You do not need to say the prayer word for word as it is stated here; feel free to make your own version. Feel free to call it the Prayer of Robin of Westfield if you would like to do so, personalize it to suit your life and needs. Also, say a plural version of *The Prayer of Jabez* for all of humanity.

The Living Well Prayer

Thank You, thank You, thank You dear Lord for all things in my life; I thank and praise You. I recognize I am a sinner;

please forgive me and cleanse me of my sins. I love You above all things; You are my Lord and Savior.

Thank You for all the blessings You have given me, such as_____(fill in with various personal blessings, ie. Your family, your education, your faith, your children, good health, etc.). Please continue to bless me indeed, giving me all Your blessings, abundance, and favors so that I may do Your will here on Earth.

Dear Lord, help me to be respectful of myself and others, to be responsible for my actions, to be honest, and to maintain a good attitude in life. Help me to be loving, forgiving, and non-judging. Help me to be positive and optimistic, to have more faith and hope in all. Help me to be more Christ-like, to be more patient, giving, kind, caring, and compassionate.

Good Lord, help me to be healthy and well, make me a magnet of your well being so I can do Your will here on Earth.

Dear Lord, use me and help me to be an instrument of Peace on earth to do Your will. Again, I thank and praise you for all; I love you above all things as You are my Lord and my God. Amen.

I hope this prayer will be useful to you or encourage you to create your own personalized prayer. We need to give thanks to our creator and know our God wants the best for us here on earth. We all need to live by our inner light, whether following the Tao Te Ching, Bible, Koran, Torah, or other spiritual sources. We must respect ourselves and each other and take responsibility for our actions and live by God's inner light in us, Emmanuel, the "God that is in us." We must live the good life of virtue. Again, like it is said in 1 Peter 1:17, "Conduct yourselves with reverence during the time of your sojourning." One of my father's favorite authors is Edgar Casey, he has always been intrigued with his insight. Casey once said, "We must live in the present. We must look at how we relate to others and our planet and take care of each so to ensure a sound future for our future and generations to come." I think this is very germane and goes back to why it is important for all of us to care enough to do what is right in this world.

So, are you who you want to be yet? It is all a work in progress; our lives and journeys always are. Our lives are a journey, not a destination. We all must strive to be good people in our journey here on earth, loving our fellow men, caring enough to do what is right for all of us here and our Mother Earth. *Living Well: Caring Enough to Do What's Right* is not about pointing fingers or being righteous. It is knowing that there is only one love that is perfect, that is the love of God. We all need to strive to live and reach this level of love. We do not want to lose our souls to gain the world of materialism and ego. Living well means loving everyone even if you do not want to. We need to love one another, we need to forgive ourselves and others, and we need to care enough to do what is right if we really want peace in our lives and world. In closing, as Henry Drummond said, "You will find, as you look back upon your life, that the moments when you have really lived are the moments when you have done things in the Spirit of love." God is good; God is love.

Joseph M. Furner

Key Idea from this Chapter:

Praying daily brings us peace. Find or create your own special prayer with God; say it and believe in it daily. Practice your faith. Recognize you are a sinner, ask God for forgiveness, and make him your Lord and Savior. Count your blessings every day for all which God has allowed you to have and achieve. Always be conscientious about having a good attitude, being ethical, being kind, and caring enough to do what is right in this world so as to make it a world of peace.

❧❧❧

I hope this libretto will help you help the world to be a more loving and peaceful place for all humankind, live well. We all must embrace the Cross which God has given us, to live with integrity, to be honest, loving, and forgiving, to work toward peace. I hope this book will help to renew your Spirit. God bless you all indeed, always!

Respectfully yours,

Joseph M. Furner, Ph.D. (God worked through me to write this book; I did not do it by myself. I must credit him, our Lord and Savior, my Source)

I would love to hear from you; please e-mail me at: peace. work@yahoo.com

❧❧❧

Copyright © by Joseph M. Furner